bible

A
BEGINNER'S
GUIDE

reading

MICHAEL GREEN

Liguori
LIGUORI, MISSOURI

Text copyright © 1999, 2009 Michael Green

Published in the United States
By Liguori Publications
1 Liguori Drive
Liguori, Missouri 63057
800-325-9521
www.liguori.org.

First published 1999 by Hodder & Stoughton Ltd
under the title *Bible Reading for Amateurs*

Published in the United Kingdom by
The Bible Reading Fellowship
15 The Chambers, Vineyard
Abingdon OX14 3FE
United Kingdom

ISBN 978-0-7648-1904-9

Copyright © 2010 The Bible Reading Fellowship

Library of Congress Cataloging-in-Publication Data

Green, Michael, 1930-
    Bible reading : a beginner's guide / Michael Green.
        p. cm.
    Rev. ed. of: Bible reading for amateurs.
    ISBN 978-0-7648-1904-9
    1. Bible—Reading. I. Green, Michael, 1930- Bible reading for amateurs. II. Title.
    BS617.G60 2010
    220.6'1—dc22

                                                                    2009038819

Acknowledgments
Scripture quotations are taken from the Holy Bible, New International Version,
copyright © 1973, 1978, 1984 by International Bible Society, are used by
permission of Hodder & Stoughton Publishers, a division of Hodder Headline
Ltd. All rights reserved. "NIV" is a registered trademark of International Bible
Society. UK trademark number 1448790.

contents

Introduction

The World's Bestseller

The Bible is far and away the world's bestseller, not just in the West but all over the world. In the days of the USSR people would risk their lives to obtain a copy. It is so powerful that today many countries ban its entry, fearful of the impact it will make. Wherever it is taken seriously, it transforms lives for the better. It is a truly amazing book.

But most ordinary men and women are profoundly ignorant of it: they never read it. It's a remarkable thing, but they may be embarrassed by it. And yet our culture has been shaped more by this book than any other single influence.

The story of the Bible is constantly being retold in historical novels, like Frederick Buechner's *The Son of Laughter* on the life of Jacob, or the bestselling Brazilian author Paulo Coehlo's *The Fifth Mountain* on the life of Elijah, or Thomas Cahill's *The Hinges of History*—a detailed retelling of events in the Old Testament. The same is taking place in film and television. Films like *Amazing Grace* and *Amistad* are dominated by the Bible. Steven Spielberg's *Prince of Egypt* is an animated portrayal of the life of Moses, while the story of Jesus comes from director after director. Think of Zeffirelli's *Jesus of Nazareth* or Mel Gibson's *The Passion of Christ*. The filmmakers cannot resist his fascination.

Funny thing, isn't it? The level of Bible knowledge in home and school is almost nil. The Christian Church seems to keep its treasure very much to itself (in a church building, on a Sunday). Its members, for the most part, do not read the Bible, and yet in the culture at large it remains the most powerful story in the world. What is this book? What is the secret of its staying power and fascination? How can we get into it and experience its impact? This book is designed to enable complete amateurs in Bible knowledge to discover its riches for themselves. We think of the word "amateur" as a non-professional of some kind, someone who isn't paid for doing his or her thing. But the root meaning of the word is "lover." I have come to love the Bible, and I hope this book will turn some of you, too, into lovers of the greatest story ever told. Read on!

one
What Is the Bible?

Not a Book, but a Library

The word "Bible" comes from a Greek word meaning "books," and that gives us a clue to start off with. We are not dealing with a single book but with a library. The Bible, in fact, consists of no fewer than 66 books. Some are long, some short. They were written over a period of more than a thousand years in three languages—Hebrew, Greek and Aramaic. They had an astonishing variety of authors, from shepherds to kings, poets to historians, prophets to warriors, mystics to fishermen.

Its Unity

If you got a bunch of people as various as that into a room and asked them their views on God and humanity, lifestyle and destiny, you would get as many answers as there were people. But the truly remarkable thing about the Bible, which justifies us in naming it as a single book, is that you find a common understanding, a unified teaching running right through it.

Always you get the same picture of God. He is the one and only author of life, the only proper object of worship. He is personal, but beyond personality. The male and female together represent something of this being. He is the source of all morality, perfect and pure and just. He is full of love for the world he has created and the people he has brought into being. The true God whom the Bible brings before us is the utterly loving but utterly incorruptible Creator.

We find, to our amazement, that we get a common understanding of human nature running through all the books of the Bible. Human beings are not gods, as some New Agers would have it. We are not just sophisticated animals, as some of the biologists maintain, or chemical constructs in motion, as some behaviorists believe. We are neither naked apes nor little angels, but are made in his image, with the ability to speak, to pray and to know the difference between right and wrong. God intended us to live in families and enjoy his company, but almost every page of the Bible reflects the fact that, down the ages, human beings have rejected that ideal. We have gone our own way, not God's way. We have pleased ourselves, not God. We have left God out of our lives and paddled our own canoe—and the chaos in human affairs all springs from that basic attitude of rebellion and disobedience. It is not just the times that are out of joint: we are. Now that is a very radical understanding of human nature and very unfashionable (although every edition of the Sunday papers underlines its truth). But it is the view on which the biblical writers are unanimous.

There is another major theme, consequent upon these two, which binds the whole Bible together. It is rescue—restoration. The Bible writers often call it "salvation." "Save" is not a word we use much nowadays, but think of someone being saved from drowning or from a burning building and you will get the idea. Both drowning and burning suggest mortal danger. That is how the Bible understands the consequences of our human rebellion. Our predicament is serious. God might well have washed his hands of us and started again, as D. H. Lawrence advised him to! But no—the Bible writers all maintain that God cares about us so much that he has found a costly way to restore us to his company and rescue us from the mess into which our self-centeredness has plunged us. This is a remarkable insight. In other faiths you find a God who is a stern judge, or who does not really care about human beings, or who is simply impersonal. The Bible tells us that God loves us so much that he was determined to do something to rescue us from the guilt our actions and attitudes bring upon us and from the grip in which our failures imprison us (Colossians 1:22).

In a word, the great theme of the Bible is "God to the rescue" (that, in fact, is the meaning of the name "Jesus"). God is Savior, the one who comes to restore the situation that we have messed up. The centerpiece of the whole story is the mindboggling claim that God came in person to this earth as Jesus. He lived a matchless life and offered that life up voluntarily on the cross as the incredibly costly way of removing our guilt, breaking our chains and making possible a way back to companionship with God. This is no mere journey "from the alone to the Alone." It involves human beings in a new community who love and seek to advance the claims of God in this world.

As if that was not enough, the Bible writers are confident that there is a future awaiting the people of God. He cares for us so much that he will not scrap us when we get old and die. He offers us a welcome in his home in heaven (Psalm 23:6). Our destiny is not to go out like a light, or to be condemned to a ceaseless round of reincarnation, but to know and enjoy forever the God who loved us and gave himself for us, and to do so in the company of all who love him and have looked to him for rescue.

That is the kernel of what the Bible is about. It would have been amazing if one person had had such improbable insights. There is no example of any single person ever coming up with anything comparable. But when all the 40 or so authors of the Bible agree in this view of God, humankind, evil, restoration, the new community and human destiny, it is simply staggering. No wonder the Bible writers claimed, and Christians have always recognized, that they were inspired. We shall look at this more closely in a later chapter. God himself gave these insights to the writers. They could never have come up with the same answers all by themselves.

So despite the many centuries over which the library of the Bible was written, despite its many authors and different languages, there is a remarkable unity that holds it all together. We have every right to see it as "the book" rather than a random collection of books embodying merely human ideas.

The Library With Two Shelves

This library of the Bible has two main parts, called the Old Testament and the New Testament. The word "testament" means "covenant" or "agreement," and the first part of the Bible enshrines the old covenant that God established with his people before he came to our world in Jesus Christ. The new covenant is the story of that coming and its significance. It brings to a climax God's self-disclosure.

To put it another way, the Old Testament is all about promise, and the New is all about fulfillment. If the Old Testament records what God spoke "in the past... to our ancestors through the prophets," the New tells us how God has "spoken to us by his Son," in whom all the older revelation is summed up, confirmed and transcended (Hebrews 1:1–2).

Just a further word of explanation to help us find our way around this large book. The Old Testament falls into three main sections, called the Law, the Prophets and the Writings. The Law comprises the first five "books of Moses." The Prophets fall into two divisions: the "former prophets," made up of

Joshua, Judges, Samuel and Kings, and the "latter prophets," comprising Isaiah, Jeremiah, Ezekiel, Daniel and a collection of twelve shorter prophecies. The Writings contain the rest of the Old Testament, and were generally written later than the Law and the Prophets.

If you think it is a bit odd to find historical books like Kings included in the Prophets, the answer is rather interesting. God reveals himself throughout the Old Testament period in two main ways—by mighty works (like the exodus from Egypt) and by prophetic words. The two belong together. God's mighty deeds of rescue and judgment would not have been intelligible unless they were interpreted by the prophets, God's "spokesmen" who received and passed on his message. This interplay of mighty deeds and prophetic word in the Old Testament explains why history and prophecy are so intermingled in its pages, and why the historical books can be seen as prophetic.

The New Testament falls naturally into four sections. First of all, there are the four Gospels, recording the story of Jesus, whose life is not only God's crowning revelation to humankind, but also humankind's perfect response to God. His coming, life, teaching, death and resurrection are brought powerfully before us in the Gospels, which were themselves an entirely new form of literature.

Then comes the Acts of the Apostles, the story of how the first Christians spread across the known world within 30 years. It makes thrilling reading. It is followed by the epistles or letters from the first Christian leaders, some to individuals and some to the churches. These letters reflect on the significance of Jesus and the implications he has for the Christian community. Finally there is a highly pictorial book, Revelation, lifting our hearts to grasp something of God's future.

So the Old Testament records the witness of those who were, consciously or unconsciously, reaching forward to God's full revelation in Jesus Christ, while the New Testament records the witness of those who saw and heard him when he was on earth, and who proclaimed far and wide the good news of who he was and what he had done for humankind. That is what the Bible is about. It's a library with a single great theme.

two
What Can It Do for Me?

What's in It for Me?

"What's in it for me?" is a very natural question, particularly in today's fast-moving society, where we are too busy to bother with anything that does not have some immediate relevance. No wonder, then, that people ask that kind of question about Bible reading: "What's the point? What can it do for me?" It can do a great deal.

What It Did for Some Skeptics

Years ago there was a young French scholar called Émile Caillet who was determined to discover truth. He turned to philosophy and spent some ten years studying all the philosophy systems that had ever been devised. He was disappointed with what he found, so he said, "I will write my own philosophy"—and he did. However, when he looked back over it some time later, he was again disappointed with what he had written. He despaired of ever finding truth.

One day he came home and found his wife reading the Bible. "Get that book of superstition out of my house," he roared. She refused. Instead, she pleaded with him at least to glance at its contents. With a bad grace he did, and he was entirely captivated by what he read. Here was the teaching which had so long eluded him and which immediately convinced him of its truth. He became a Christian. In due course his biblical studies led him to become a theologian. Indeed, he spent many fruitful years as a professor at Princeton Seminary in the USA. Looking back on the whole experience, he said, "At last I have found a book which understands me."

The Bible has always had this life-changing power. In the early days of the Church, a very able intellectual, Justin, was treading much the same path as Émile Caillet. He had studied the Platonic, Aristotelian and Cynic philosophical systems of the ancient world and, like Caillet, he was disappointed because none of them had the ring of truth about them that he was looking for. One day he met an old man in the fields, who, seeing his philosopher's cloak, asked him what the true philosophy was. Justin was, of course, unable to give a satisfactory reply because he had not found it himself. So the old man asked him to read and reflect on a copy of the Scriptures. Justin did so, reluctantly, and he was never the same again. He found that the

Scriptures "possess a terrible power in themselves" and also "a wonderful sweetness," which made an incredible impression on him. He became a follower of Jesus. He refused to lay aside his philosopher's cloak but fearlessly proclaimed the "true philosophy" that he found in the Scriptures throughout his life, until he was dragged off to a martyr's death. He saw those same Scriptures lead his pupil Athenagoras to Christ. Both of them figure among the major Christian thinkers of the second century, and both of them were won by the powerful truth they found in the Scriptures. The Bible is a life-changing book. That is what it can do for you!

When Charles Darwin first visited the Galapagos Islands on the Beagle in 1835, he found that the inhabitants were utterly dejected and corrupt. He was very depressed by their abysmal condition. When he went back years later, after the first missionaries had brought the Scriptures there, he was so fascinated by the transformation of the people that he became a lifelong subscriber to what became the South American Missionary Society.

Charles Dickens put the matter very succinctly: "The New Testament is the best book the world has ever known and will ever know." "It is more than a book to me," reflected Napoleon, in exile on St. Helena. "It is, as it were, a person." It has an astonishing power to address us personally, as if it were written for us alone. "It is talking to me and about me," said the Danish philosopher, Søren Kierkegaard. Perhaps that is why no skeptical criticism, no persecution, no confiscation, no sanctions against reading this book have ever succeeded. Its sales just go on growing: there is no other book in the same league.

But let's be specific. What can it do for you?

What Can It Do for Me?

First and foremost, it can change your life. Not that it has any magical powers, but it puts you in touch with the living God who can give you spiritual life just as he has given you natural life. The written word can put you in touch with Jesus, the living Word (or self-disclosure) of God. Just as you can only know my unseen thoughts if I clothe them in words, so we can only know the unseen God if he communicates to us in words we can take in. That he has done. As the American evangelist D. L. Moody put it, "The Bible was not given to increase our knowledge. It was given to change our lives."

Once people start reading it with an open heart, God is able to get through to them. John's Gospel embodies that claim very clearly. He tells us why he wrote his book. It was so "that you may believe that Jesus is the Christ, the Son of God, and that by believing you may have life in his name" (John 20:31).

Notice the two stages in that purpose. The first one is calculated to show the reader what John himself discovered by personal companionship with Jesus—that he really is the Son of God. John gives us in his Gospel seven great signs that Jesus did, followed by the supreme sign of his death and resurrection. These convinced John himself, and he records them for others so that they may see solid grounds for belief. But it can never rest there. Jesus is the one who gives a new dimension to life—a spiritual rebirth, no less. That is what John wants for his readers, that they may have "life in his name." He tells us that Jesus proclaimed, "I have come that they may have life, and have it to the full" (John 10:10).

There are many other things that the Bible can do for us. Once we have discovered the new life in Christ, Scripture is able to build us up and show us more and more of the treasures we have inherited as Christians (Acts 20:32). It is a gradual process. We are not dropped into the deep end all at once. While there are lots of things we shall not understand, there is plenty that we can readily take on board and find really nourishing—particularly in the Gospels and Psalms. The Bible calls itself milk, milk for babies in the Christian life. Peter writes to new believers, "Like newborn babies, crave pure spiritual milk, so that by it you may grow" (1 Peter 2:2).

Of course, we are not meant to stay at that level for long, but to develop. Wouldn't it be disappointing if a nursing baby never got on to solid food? Accordingly, the Bible also compares itself to meat for those who are mature. Paul has reason to complain of some of the Christians at Corinth, whom he himself had led to Christ, "I gave you milk, not solid food, for you were not yet ready for it. Indeed, you are still not ready" (1 Corinthians 3:2). Sadly, that is true of so many Christians today. They are semi-starved. They have not been built up in their spiritual lives by the Scriptures.

The Bible gives us a deep insight into Jesus himself, and there is no substitute for that. Hear Dr. Christopher Chavasse, a saintly bishop of Rochester in days gone by:

> *The Bible is the portrait of our Lord Jesus Christ. The Gospels are the figure itself in the portrait. The Old Testament is the background leading up to the divine figure, pointing towards it and absolutely necessary to the composition as a whole. The Epistles serve as the dress and equipment of the figure, explaining and describing it. Then, while by our Bible reading we study the portrait as a whole, the miracle happens and the figure comes to life. Stepping down from the canvas of the written word, the everlasting Christ of the Emmaus story becomes himself our Bible teacher, to interpret to us in all the Scriptures the things concerning himself.*

That may be language of 70 years ago, but the meaning is both clear and helpful. Martin Luther put it in a memorable way: "As we come to the cradle only to find the baby, so we come to the Scriptures only to find the Christ."

The Bible's Own Claims

The Bible itself contains some marvelous images of what it can do. It is like a fire, to warm our hearts when they are cold. "'Is not my word like fire,' declares the Lord, 'and like a hammer that breaks a rock in pieces?'" (Jeremiah 23:29). I don't know about you, but my heart is often both cold and rock-like. I need to have that rock broken up, that fire lit. That is what Scripture can do when we come to it humbly.

Here is something else. The Bible is described as the sword that the Holy Spirit uses to fight for us in times of temptation (Ephesians 6:17). The classic example of this is the use Jesus himself made of some verses he seems to have committed to memory from the book of Deuteronomy. When fiercely tempted in the wilderness, he faced each temptation with the words "It is written…" (Matthew 4:1–11). In each case, that "sword of the Spirit" drove the tempter away. Try it. It works!

No wonder the prophet Ezekiel saw the portion of the Scriptures that had been written in his day as something wonderfully sweet. "He said to me, '… eat this scroll I am giving you and fill your stomach with it.' So I ate it, and it tasted as sweet as honey in my mouth" (Ezekiel 3:3). Bizarre imagery, perhaps, but wonderfully clear teaching! The psalmist, too, was so thrilled with God's word through the Scriptures that he created an elaborate psalm, every verse of which sings of one of the splendors of God's revelation. (That, by the way, is Psalm 119, the longest psalm in the book.) He certainly found it sweet and nourishing to his soul, and so will we if only we will start reading a bit of it on a daily basis. It will build us up and be "a lamp to our feet and a light for our path" (Psalm 119:105). We all need a bit of illumination and guidance in the problems that beset us daily, and you will be amazed to find that in your daily reading you often get just the insight and direction that you were looking for.

John Wesley certainly discovered the truth of this, and it might be good to end this chapter with his passionate outburst:

I want to know one thing, the way to heaven. God himself condescended to teach that way. For this very end he came from heaven. He has written it down in a book. O give me that book, at any price, give me that book! If I have it, there is knowledge enough for me. Let me be a man of one book!

three
How Shall I Approach It?

What Is the Bible for?

There used to be a book on my shelves called *The Bible as Literature.* I do not have it any longer. You see, the Bible is magnificent literature. It is the greatest literature in the world, and the old King James version is a highlight of English prose (which is why some agnostics are still so keen to retain it). But it was not designed to be read or valued simply for its literary quality.

There still is a book on my shelves entitled *The Bible as History.* I have not disposed of it during my various house moves for two good reasons. It has a lot of valuable material in it, and the Bible is historically reliable. Every discovery in archaeology vindicates the accuracy of the biblical account. But the Bible is not primarily intended to be a history book. It contains history, but it is much more than that.

There is a third way of looking at the Bible that is very common. It is seen as inspirational. It gives us inspiring thoughts from spiritually gifted human beings about God and the good life. To be sure, it was written by people in close touch with God and it does tell us about how life should be lived. That is not what the Bible is about, however. It is not the product of inspiring people. It is not comparable to inspiring masterpieces like Shakespeare's *Hamlet* or Handel's *Messiah*. It claims to be (with very good reason, as we shall see in a later chapter) "breathed out" by God. He breathed out the material we have in the Bible, and a variety of human authors were sufficiently in touch with God to assimilate it and write it down for the benefit of humankind.

In a letter to his friend Timothy, the apostle Paul says, "From infancy you have known the holy Scriptures, which are able to make you wise for salvation through faith in Christ Jesus. All Scripture is God-breathed and is useful for teaching, rebuking, correcting and training in righteousness, so that God's servant may be thoroughly equipped for every good work" (2 Timothy 3:15–17). That is what the Bible is for. It is revelation breathed out by God, not bright ideas about God dreamed up by men and women. It is God's self-disclosure, not human speculation.

As such, it is immensely profitable. It is profitable for teaching us about God and about life, for rebuking us when we need it, for correcting us when we have gone wrong, and for training us in the Christian life so that we may go deep and become mature and a blessing to society.

If that is why God gave us the Bible, it suggests to me a number of important attitudes that I need to adopt as I come to read it.

How Shall I Approach the Bible?

First, I shall want to approach it humbly. If Scripture really is designed by God to teach us what we need to know about him, for our good and the good of others, then it is obvious that you and I must come to it humbly. Some Christian leaders in the New Testament are charmingly described as "servants of the word" (Luke 1:2). That is the right attitude. I am not over the Bible, to judge it and decide what bits I shall accept and what bits I can reject. I am under the word. I need to let it judge me, if necessary. I need to listen reflectively to what it is saying and see how it applies to my life. It is astonishing how blind some highly intelligent but proud people can be to what the Bible is saying to them. It is equally astonishing to see the spiritual insight gained by utterly uneducated people who come humbly to the Scriptures, saying, in effect, "Speak, Lord, for your servant is listening." Saint Augustine came to recognize that the Scriptures are "letters from home," but he had not always seen them in that light. Before his conversion, he tells us, he was dissatisfied with pagan philosophers like Cicero and resolved to turn to the Bible in search of wisdom. "But I did not understand it, because I came with pride. The

Bible is a book for those who come to it humbly." That is how I need to approach it.

Second, I need to come expectantly. Most of all, I want to meet the living Word within the written word. I want to meet Christ in the pages before me. It is rather like a correspondence between a pair of lovers. When she gets a letter from him, she reads it eagerly, mulling over the words and suggestions. She reads it again, commits bits of it to heart. It is not the letters on the page that thrill her but the person of her lover that those letters bring to her. Bible reading can be deadly dull if you read it as history, literature or bright ideas about God from religious people. But it becomes as thrilling as any love letter when you seek to meet your Lord in its pages.

One of the most remarkable spiritual leaders of the 20th century was Archbishop Anthony Bloom. A Russian émigré, he was aggressively anti-Christian in his youth. He hated the very idea of God. Indeed, convinced that life had no meaning, he was contemplating suicide. Then one day he was forced to listen to a Christian priest. It made him furious and he went home to read one of the Gospels in order to prove the man wrong. He selected Mark because it was the shortest. He tells us, "Before I reached the third chapter I suddenly became aware that on the other side of my desk there was a presence. And the certainty was so strong that it was Christ standing there that it has never left me. This was the real turning point." He became successively a doctor, a priest and an archbishop, but it all began when he met

Christ himself in the pages of the Gospel. He was not expecting anything of the sort at the time—but he did so for the rest of his life, and we should follow his example.

Third, I must approach the Bible honestly. I shall find difficulties that I cannot explain. Sometimes they will be intellectual difficulties, like how Jesus could be both Son of God and a human being. Sometimes I will find philosophical difficulties, like the possibility of miracles, and sometimes moral difficulties, especially in the Old Testament, where God commands the Jews to slaughter the Amalakites who could infect them with idolatry and immorality.

So I suggest you keep a mental pending tray! Put problems like that in the tray and talk them over, when opportunity offers, with some wise Christian friend who knows more than you do. Don't let what you don't understand ruin what you do understand, or you will gain no profit from your Bible reading.

Suppose you were served a beautifully cooked trout for your meal. Would you carefully separate the bones from the flesh, and then struggle to swallow the bones while leaving the flesh aside? Of course not. You would put the bones on the side of the plate and tuck into the meat. Do that with your Bible reading—but never pretend to yourself that there are no real problems; do not leave them unexamined. You have to handle the Bible with the utmost intellectual honesty, but do not allow your devotional time with the Bible to be spoiled because you are gnawing away at the bones rather than feasting on the flesh. Keep the bones until later.

Fourth, it is wise to come to the Bible imaginatively. I sometimes try to put myself into the shoes of someone I have just read about in the story. For example, I try to recapture what it must have felt like when Jesus fed 5,000 people from a few small loaves. What would I have written in my diary when I staggered back home, footsore but awestruck, at the end of such a day? Or I wonder how I would have reacted to hearing the letter to the Philippians for the very first time as the messenger, Epaphroditus, sweating from his long journey, read it aloud to our Christian group packed into a house in the garrison town of Philippi.

Please note that I am not advocating wild, uncontrolled flights of fancy—they can lead you all over the place! What I am encouraging you to do is to allow your God-given imagination to engage with the biblical text. It will help to make your Bible reading spring to life.

Fifth, I shall want to read the Bible attentively. It is no good rushing into a hastily chosen Bible passage, spinning through it and expecting to get something from it. That would be as useless as seeing a nice meal on your plate and sparing time only to lick the gravy or grab a potato on the run. I need to make time to read, and then to read the same piece again more slowly and allow the Lord to make something come alive for me.

You know how it is at Christmas in the street, with colored lights up everywhere. You hardly notice them in the daytime; they look dull and useless. When they are switched on in the evening, though, it is entirely different. God will switch on the lights for us and make some thought from the Scripture luminous to us, if we take time in his presence, read attentively and ask him to meet with us.

Sixth, I need to approach the Bible obediently. We read in the letter of James:

> *Do not merely listen to the word, and so deceive yourselves. Do what it says. Those who listen to the word but do not do what it says are like people who look at their faces in a mirror and, after looking at themselves, go away and immediately forget what they look like. But those who look intently into the perfect law that gives freedom, and continue to do this, not forgetting what they have heard, but doing it—they will be blessed in what they do.*

JAMES 1:22–25

A good point, isn't it? You would never dream of looking at your face in the mirror, seeing a great smudge and doing nothing about it. You would act. You would wipe it off. That is what you and I are meant to do when we read a bit of Scripture. We need to apply it to our lives, and act.

Finally, I must come to it regularly. I do not look in the mirror once a week and hope that all will be well the rest of the time. I look in the mirror at least once a day. I do not have a massive lunch on Sunday and starve for the rest of the week. I like my lunch every day. Very well, then, I should make a regular daily meal of my Bible reading. It can have an enormous impact on our lives if we come to it regularly and allow it to affect the way we behave. It is life-transforming, no less.

I could cite a number of examples of the remarkable power this book has to change us for the better, but here is one from a particularly difficult part of the world—Cuba. The Cuban Bible Commission relate how they gave a Bible to a young prisoner called Armando. He was a complete rebel against society. His heart was full of bitterness. They were amazed that he accepted the Bible, but he did and began to read it. "With every visit," they said, "we saw his faith growing in leaps and bounds." Armando abandoned his bad behavior and improved his attitude so much that he started to be known in the prison for his exemplary conduct. Today Armando is back outside, and now he is the one who takes his family to church. His former acquaintances are amazed at the dramatic new turn his life has taken.

four
How Can I Begin?

"The only secret about this change lies in the Bible. It brought light into his prison cell and helped him transform his life to the point where he was leading other prisoners to God while still serving his sentence."

Such is the transforming power of the word of God when we read and apply it regularly.

If you were going out to a meal with a friend, you would certainly make some preparations: a wash and brush-up, a comb through the hair, perhaps a change of clothes. Why should it be any different when we set out to meet with God?

Preparations

- **Get alone with God:** John Wesley, who was the key figure in the 18th-century Christian revival that probably saved England from revolution, used to get up to spend his daily time with God at 4:00 AM—putting me to shame! But I imagine he was able to get some privacy at that time of day. He wrote, "I sit down alone….Only God is here. In his presence I open, I read his book. And what I read I teach." Unless you find a place where you can be alone, it can be extremely hard to concentrate.

- **Get a regular time:** It is helpful to find a regular time of day when you can focus on God. Our lives are so full that unless we build a regular spot, we shall find that it simply does not happen. I know this is so—I have failed so often in this respect. Many people find the morning the best time, before everything else crowds in.

- **Get a Bible translation you can enjoy:** There is nothing to beat the King James Bible for beauty of language, but it is nearly 400 years old and not altogether easy to understand. So find one of the modern translations that you like. Either Today's New International Version or the Contemporary English Version would be an excellent choice.

- **Get right with God:** Do you remember your mother calling you in to dinner when you were young? "Dinner's ready. Come and wash your hands!" That was wise advice and it holds good for our time with God. We need to wash our hands first. We need to come to him and ask him to show us anything in our lives that has grieved him, confess it and realize with deep gratitude that "if we confess our sins, God is faithful and just and will forgive us our sins and purify us from all unrighteousness" (1 John 1:9).

- **Get "online":** You know how it is with your computer. You can type away on email to your heart's content but it only communicates to anybody else when you get online, and that requires a definite act on your part. Well, that has something to teach us. God's written word alone will not really communicate with us until we are "online" with God and ask him to make it come alive and speak to us through it. Before we start reading, we might find it helpful to use a short prayer, like the psalmist: "Open my eyes that I may see wonderful things in your law" (Psalm 119:18).

The Time Together

Naturally, the first thing to do is to read the passage you have chosen slowly a couple of times and see what strikes you. You will want to be clear on the main point of the passage, and then you will find it helpful to ask two questions.

Questions

First, ask "What did this mean to the original recipients?" and second, "If it meant that to them, what can it mean to me today?"

If you don't ask the first question, you can read all sorts of things into Scripture that were never intended by the writers. If you don't ask the second, you can find yourself in a desert of dry intellectual information that does nothing for your Christian life. Both questions are needed.

Some subsidiary questions are a great help in getting at the heart of the passage. I find it helpful to ask myself some questions such as these:

- Is there something new about God that I can see in this passage?
- Is there some example for me to follow?
- Is there some warning for me to heed?
- Is there a command to obey?
- Is there a promise to claim?
- Is there some fresh insight into the daily problems that I face?
- What shall I take away as a "thought for the day"?

Reflection

As you go through those questions and apply them to what you have read, some of them will probably be irrelevant. For example, there may be no warnings or promises in the passage you are looking at. But you are getting into the helpful habit of asking questions of the text and letting it speak to you. That is the important thing. Some of those questions will certainly relate to what you have read, so let them be your gateways into the text. You may even like to use a notebook to jot down what you have found helpful.

Prayer

Now is the time to reflect, meditate on what you have read, and turn it into prayer and praise. Remember, you should be looking for a two-way conversation—God most certainly is. He wants to hear from you in response to what he puts before you. Get into the way of praying over what you have read—praying it into your heart and life.

Bible Reading Aids

In the next chapter we will explore how your time together with the Lord might be developed. But before I close this one I want to introduce you to one of the Bible reading aids that are readily available. You can buy Bible reading notes from most Christian bookshops or direct from the publishers. Taking out a subscription is a good way of making sure you always have the latest issues at hand. A passage of Scripture is chosen for each day (sometimes printed out in the notes themselves) with helpful comments, usually followed by a prayer or a thought for the day. Here is a typical one for you to sample:

Ephesians 1:3–14 (TNIV)

An Outpouring of Praise

Praise be to the God and Father of our Lord Jesus Christ, who has blessed us in the heavenly realms with every spiritual blessing in Christ.

The first three chapters of this letter are a wonderful intermingling of praise, intercession and doctrine. As we look at Paul's outpouring in prayer in these chapters, we will see the strands woven together.

What is the most memorable waterfall you have ever seen? The Victoria Falls in Zambia or the Niagara Falls in Canada? High Force in Teesdale or Aira Force in the Lake District? The water cascades with endless power in fascinating patterns. Paul's praise is like that as his wonder at the richness of God's blessing tumbles out—all in one long sentence in the original Greek. He is full of joy at God's lavish generosity. So what does he see as the cause for such praise?

God chose us (vv. 4, 11) long before we ever chose to follow him. He chose us "before the creation of the world": isn't that amazing? He chose us to live holy lives: what a standard!

He adopted us as his children (v. 5). It is as if God picked us up as street kids and made us part of his royal family.

He redeems us (v. 7). The image here is of a pawnbroker. The rightful owner, God the Father, has bought us back at the immense cost of Jesus' death, "through his blood." He enlightened us (v. 9) and has shown us his eternal purposes. He included us "in Christ" (v. 13), with all the privileges of that relationship. He sealed us with the Holy Spirit (v. 13). A seal was a mark of ownership, of personal identification, so we belong to him. The Spirit is also a deposit guaranteeing more to come, like the down-payment we may make on the purchase of a car—a promise of full payment in the future.

> *Think how impoverished we would be if God had not chosen us—if he had left us in the gutter, abandoned us in the shop, left us in the dark, with no understanding and no Holy Spirit to give us life within. Then join in Paul's praise and use it as your own prayer.*

DAY BY DAY WITH GOD, SEPTEMBER–DECEMBER 2008
ROSEMARY GREEN (BRF/CHRISTINA PRESS), 45

Bible reading notes like these, taking you through books of the Bible in short, easy-to-assimilate passages, have a lot to commend them. But let me give you a warning. Don't read the notes until you have gotten "online" with God yourself and seen what you can find in the passage. Otherwise it can all be rather second-hand, and that is a disaster in any relationship!

five
How Can I Get the Best Out of It?

I promised in the last chapter that you and I would dig into a passage of Scripture together and see what we could find, so let's go for it. Suppose we are due to look at Psalm 27 in the course of our reading.

The alarm goes off and, because we have placed it quite deliberately out of reach, we have to get up to turn the wretched thing off. Cold water works wonders on sleepy faces, and before long we are dressed, more or less in our right mind and with a cup of coffee in our hand. We see that Psalm 27 beckons. We put the coffee down and reverently ask the Lord to cleanse us from anything we have failed to confess to him, so that there is no blockage in our time together. Then we ask him to shine his light on the page so that it leaps to life for us. Then we read slowly through the psalm.

1. The Lord is my light and my salvation—whom shall I fear? The Lord is the stronghold of my life—of whom shall I be afraid?

2. When the wicked advance against me to devour my flesh, when my enemies and my foes attack me, they will stumble and fall.

3. Though an army besiege me, my heart will not fear; though war break out against me, even then will I be confident.

4. One thing I ask of the Lord, this is what I seek: that I may dwell in the house of the Lord all the days of my life, to gaze upon the beauty of the Lord and to seek him in his temple.

5. For in the day of trouble he will keep me safe in his dwelling; he will hide me in the shelter of his tabernacle and set me high upon a rock.

6. Then my head will be exalted above the enemies who surround me; at his tabernacle will I sacrifice with shouts of joy; I will sing and make music to the Lord.

7. Hear my voice when I call, O Lord; be merciful to me and answer me.

8. To you, O my heart, he has said, "Seek my face!" Your face, Lord, I will seek.

9. Do not hide your face from me, do not turn your servant away in anger; you have been my helper. Do not reject me or forsake me, O God my Savior.

10. Though my father and mother forsake me, the Lord will receive me.

11. Teach me your way, O Lord; lead me in a straight path because of my oppressors.
12. Do not hand me over to the desire of my foes, for false witnesses rise up against me, breathing out violence.
13. I am still confident of this: I will see the goodness of the Lord in the land of the living.
14. Wait for the Lord; be strong and take heart and wait for the Lord.

Let's read it over one more time, slowly. It is not difficult to see what the psalm is about. It was written by King David in the midst of the many troubles of his reign, and it expresses his deep confidence in the Lord, come what may. That's not a bad tip for my life, as well. So I'll turn it into a prayer:

Lord, please give me the deep underlying confidence in you that David had.

Now, let's see how the psalm is made up. The first three verses reflect on the Lord's reliability, the second three on David's resolve, and then it moves into prayer from verses 7 to 12, ending with a final expression of confidence in the Lord. Reflection, prayer, confidence—a good pattern for me to pick up from time to time. I think I'll jot that down in my notebook for today.

Is there, I wonder, something new about God that I can see in this passage? Yes—in fact, I don't need to go beyond the first verse. I can imagine David rejoicing in God as his light in the dark and his savior in tough times, but those things are not only true for David. The Lord is my light, not just other people's. Light—that's worth pondering on. It is light that makes things grow. It is light that brings joy after a dark night. Light shows the way and is a beacon in the gloom. There's a lot in this concept of light—but God is also my light. I know him and trust him: I have this personal relationship with him. That is wonderful. May I never take it for granted.

He is my salvation, too. I'm not quite sure what that means but it is clearly all to do with rescue and wholeness. I am glad God is my salvation. I'm going to tell him so:

Lord, it is wonderful to think of you as my light and my salvation. Thank you with all my heart.

Right, is there some example for me to follow? There are several, I think. David's attitude in this psalm has a lot to teach me, but I am amazed in particular by verse 8. It seems that David is becoming aware that God wants him to "seek his face," and David's glad and eager response is, "Your face, Lord, I will seek." It is simply astonishing that the Lord of heaven and earth should invite human beings into his company and should actually want to have us in touch with him. It is no less astonishing how slow we are (at any rate, I am) to take advantage of this gracious offer. After all, if I had an invitation from the Queen saying, in effect,

"Seek my face," I would jump at it with enthusiasm. Why, then, am I so reluctant to get out of bed in the morning to meet the King of kings? I have a lot to learn from David's response.

Lord, I don't think I had quite realized the enormous privilege it is to have an audience with you. I hadn't seen that you were longing to meet me. May this go deep into my heart and motivate me to get out of bed to meet you, especially when I am reluctant to do so on a cold morning.

Is there some warning to heed? I don't think there is. So what else should I look for? Ah yes, is there some fresh insight into the daily problems we face? Well, there seems to be a lot in the psalm about that. There are several references to the enemies and dangers besetting King David. He speaks of "the wicked," "enemies and foes" (a whole "army" of them), "trouble," "rejection," "oppressors" and "false witnesses." I need not kid myself that it was easier for people to lead a godly life in those far-off days. I don't have an army coming to attack me, but I certainly have my enemies. I have the false witnesses who spread untrue gossip about me at work. I know both trouble and rejection, so can I learn anything from David's reactions? Well, verse 2 suggests that enemies are to be expected. I should not be surprised when this happens to me. Second, he seems to have conquered the fear factor (v. 3). His confidence really is in the Lord. Third, he describes God's protection in a marvelous way. It is as if he hides us deep in a safe cave or puts us on top of some great rock where the waves cannot reach us. Those are lovely pictures— worth thinking about.

> *Lord, I panic so easily when trouble comes or when I get slandered. Please help me not to be surprised by this sort of thing and to experience the confidence you can give in place of fear. And please keep me safe through the pressures that I realize are bound to come. Because, Lord, I do want to be a credit to you.*

What about a promise? Is there one here? Oh yes, verse 10. "Though my father and mother forsake me, the Lord will receive me." That really is something! My parents would give the clothes off their backs for me but, even if they were to disown me, the Lord will receive me. That's amazing generosity.

> *Lord, I find that promise overwhelming. Thank you so much.*

Is there, I wonder, a prayer that I could make my own? Yes, verse 11 is superb. "Teach me your way, O Lord." All too often I pray, "Bless the way I have chosen, O Lord," but this is much better. The Lord knows what is best for my life. I need to ask him to have his will with me, not to bless my will.

> *Lord, keep me praying that your will may be done in my life, not mine.*

It's time for breakfast and then off to work, but is there something I can take away and reflect on at odd moments in the day? Maybe it could be verse 4. King David clearly longed to spend time in the "house of the Lord" for the twin purposes of simply gazing on his beauty and bringing requests to him. I don't need to go into a building for that (though it might be no bad idea to nip into that church nearby for five minutes at lunch time). But I do want to keep close to the Lord so that I can enjoy his presence and bring needs to him at any time. No, good as that is, it is all too much of a mouthful to take away as a thought for the day. I can't do better than the final verse: "Wait for the Lord." I am so impetuous, so reluctant to wait, but time and again I have discovered that although the good Lord often cuts it fine, he is never late. Lord, I'm going to wait for you today!

> *Lord God, this has been a really helpful time with you this morning. May it show in how I behave today. Please keep me looking to you for courage if the going gets rough. Thank you so much that you are my light and my salvation. I really do want to keep close to you so that I can simply enjoy your beauty and bring my requests to you. And Lord, please guide me today—I really do want your way, not mine.*

This is not very sophisticated Bible study; it is the response of an amateur, a lover, to the Lord who says to us, "Seek my face!" It's no bad way to proceed.

six
How Can I Avoid Getting Stale?

One of the dangers in Bible reading is boredom. If you do the same thing in the same way day after day in any walk of life, you run the risk of getting bored. Why should it be any different with reading the Bible? The approach we looked at in the last couple of chapters is a valuable servant if you want to get regular spiritual food from the Bible, but it is a bad master if it leads to boredom.

Variety is what is needed. There are more ways than one to read the Bible profitably. In this chapter we shall examine two of them.

Read a Whole Book

Naturally you will not have leisure to read a whole book of the Bible very often, but occasionally it can be very refreshing. After all, the books of the Bible were not designed to be read in ten-verse portions. You gain an overview of the purpose of the book as a whole when you give yourself time to read it through at a sitting.

Maybe begin with a very short letter, like Philemon, which would have been written on just one page of papyrus. Ask yourself who wrote it, to whom and why, which are all good questions. In this case it is clear who wrote the letter: the apostle Paul. He wrote it to one of his own converts, Philemon, and the house church he led. Philemon appears to have been a landowner whose slave, Onesimus, had stolen money, run away and been imprisoned. Onesimus' companion in prison was none other than the apostle Paul, who found himself incarcerated for his faith. Well, Paul led this runaway slave to Christ, and now he is writing to ask Philemon to forgive Onesimus and have him back, once he is released from prison. This would have been an unheard-of thing in the ancient world: runaway slaves were crucified if they were caught. Moreover, Paul wants Philemon not to have Onesimus back as a slave but to welcome him as a beloved Christian brother. What an astonishing letter! It spells social revolution and the end of distinctions between slave and free. Just think what dynamics are released when both master and slave are brought to Christ. There is great power to change society in this book you are reading.

A while ago, I came across a remarkable example of this power to change. Dr. Mae Alice Reggy, as a Bible Society consultant, told of a practice among the villagers of north Ghana. When a family was deep in debt they would often settle it by giving one of their daughters as a slave to the juju or fetish priest. These girls were regularly abused and raped. When the Christian workers first arrived, they taught these girls literacy and then gave them Bibles in their own Éwé dialect. This resulted in many conversions: the girls came to see how much God valued them. They began to escape from the fetish priests, who resorted to their traditional magic in order to restrain them—but it did not work on Christian girls. Soon, more girls began to leave. This attracted attention from the media. The girls said on camera, "We have learned to read and we have read about Jesus. Now we are Christians and we are leaving this old way of life for a new one." The fetish priests, of course, accused the girls of rebelling against their culture. A lively debate ensued, but the outcome was that the government abolished the practice, returned the girls to their homes and outlawed human bondage as a way of settling debts. Today, as in the first century, whole communities can be changed by the power of God's word.

Liberation, then, is clearly the main point of this letter to Philemon. As you read it over again, though, you cannot help being struck by a number of other things: the great courtesy and tact of the apostle, his refusal to lay down the law to Philemon (instead he appeals to his better nature), the emphasis on hospitality, the importance of the church in the home, the humor, the love, the passion for evangelism even in prison, and a lot more. You could have a fascinating time of discovery as you range over the 25 verses of this short letter.

Now think of a rather longer letter in the New Testament, the first letter of Peter. It is full of profound material so we tend to read it in very small bits. But it is also good to read it at a single sitting and see its very clear overview. Peter wrote it to Christians scattered around the eastern Mediterranean to encourage them at a time when they were suffering a good deal of unpopularity because of their stand as Christians, which had led to fierce opposition and harassment from their colleagues at work. If you are facing ostracism or even harassment in your work or social life because you are a Christian, it might be invaluable to stand back from the situation a little and see it through the lens of this letter, written to provide encouragement to Christians long ago in a similar situation.

Or suppose you feel overwhelmed at the sheer nastiness of life today, with its human corruption, unceasing wars, famines, disasters and the threat of international terrorism. Why not take a leisurely read through the book of Revelation? You won't understand it all, any more than you "understand" an intricate sonata or a complicated painting, but let the main point of it grab you. The main point is very obvious. The apostle John is writing to Christian communities in various key cities which are going through apocalyptic times under a totalitarian regime, and he wants to show them the true realities of the situation. He wants to take them behind the scenes into God's control room, so to speak, and help them to realize that the Lord God omnipotent really is reigning, despite appearances. In the graphic wording of the book of Revelation, "the Lamb who was slain" is "in the centre of the throne" of God (5:6, 12). Ultimate victory is assured: it is God, not pain, death and disaster, who will have the last word. No wonder this book has been so prized by persecuted Christians the world over.

Or maybe you are just feeling fed up. You have been a Christian for some time and you are reluctant to get involved in some area of service to God, which you know perfectly well you should do. How about reading the book of Jonah at a sitting? Jonah felt just like you. He intended to travel as far away as he could from God's purpose for his life, and God went to extraordinary lengths to bring him back on track. Once he returned to the path of obedience, he found out how happy and fulfilling it was. Highly relevant stuff, is it not?

The book of Judges speaks very directly to our postmodern society, where we all want to "do our own thing." It tells us about a society where everyone "did what was right in their own eyes" (21:25, NRSV). The result was chaotic and God's people were overwhelmed by a variety of enemies and disasters. In successive generations, however, when they cried to the Lord for help and really meant it, he answered them and raised up leader after leader to deliver them.

Reading a whole book, long or short, in one go is without doubt a very useful variation in Bible reading. Here is another, which takes a quite different approach.

Immerse Yourself in a Single Verse

Just as a miner will sometimes strike a particularly rich vein, so in Bible reading you sometimes come across such a profound verse that it merits your full attention for the time you have at your disposal. For example, 1 Peter 3:18 is all about what the death of Jesus means for us, and has great depth of meaning. This is what it says: "For Christ died for sins once for all, the righteous for the unrighteous, to bring you to God."

Think about that for a moment, concentrating on each word or phrase. In the previous verses, Peter has been talking about innocent suffering, and that leads him on to the supreme example of innocent suffering, where the best person who ever lived died one of the cruelest deaths ever invented.

Who was this awesome sufferer? It was the Christ, God's anointed one, the climax of God's revelation, the one who had been so longed for and anticipated by prophets and people of faith down the centuries.

Was it easy for him to go to the cross? Not at all. It involved the most excruciating suffering and culminated in death by crucifixion, the most shameful form of execution in the Roman world.

Why, then, did Jesus do it? He went to the cross not because he wanted to make some grand heroic gesture, not because the Mafia caught up with him, not to show how much God loved us (how could torturing his Son show that?). No, he went there "for sins," not his own but the sins of the whole world.

'Well," you may say, "I still don't understand that sort of talk.

What does it mean?" It means, says Peter, that he, the righteous one, stood in for us, the unrighteous ones. I can't quarrel with that description either of him or of us—can you? It was "the righteous for the unrighteous." It must mean, then, that Christ voluntarily underwent our doom, carried our burden, expunged our guilt—and it cost him his life to do it. Amazing grace indeed!

"But that was a long time ago. Does something of the sort not need repeating?" It does not. His death for the rescue of human-kind was "once for all." It never needs repeating. However many human beings there have been or ever will be, their number is still finite. The self sacrifice of the God-man Jesus Christ was infinite. It provided salvation for Abraham centuries before Christ was born. It provides salvation for you and me, centuries after.

It is not automatic in its operation, however. The whole purpose of the cross, Peter tells us, was "to bring you to God." God is alienated by all the evil in my life and yours. On the cross, that alienation was abolished for those who allow Jesus to bring them to his heavenly Father. The purpose of the "at-one-ment" (which is what the technical term "atonement" means) is achieved when we let Christ cleanse us and bring us to the Father's presence— "ransomed, healed, restored, forgiven," as the hymn writer Henry Lyte put it. What a lot there is in that single verse!

Now apply that method of digging deep into the text to something like Paul's great motto: "I want to know Christ and the power of his resurrection and the fellowship of sharing in his sufferings, becoming like him in his death, and so, somehow, to attain to the resurrection from the dead" (Philippians 3:10–11).

Notice the supreme aim of this old Christian warrior: "to know Christ." That is what Christianity is all about. "But," we might ask him, "did you not get to know Christ years ago on the Damascus road?" "Indeed I did," he would reply. "But that was only the beginning of our relationship—the introduction, so to speak. I want to go on to know him more and more." If we press Paul on what that would involve, he has a clear answer for us. It will mean "the power of his resurrection." He wants to see God releasing in our frail mortal lives the very same power that raised Christ from the grave. Reflect on the moral transformation and spiritual dynamism that that suggests.

There is nothing triumphalist about Christianity, though. We are bound to experience suffering as well as victory. Paul knows that "the fellowship of sharing in his sufferings," in hardship, rejection and illness, is a great way to deepen the intimacy with Christ that he craves. There must, in fact, be a conscious and daily dying to the old life and a rising to the new life if we are to develop healthy Christian lives. We will have to "become like him in his death." And somehow it will all end with our sharing in "the resurrection from the dead," which Jesus pioneered, a magnificent and profound goal for any Christian to pursue.

What we have done in this chapter is to take a telescope and a magnifying glass to our Bible study. The first has given us an overview of what we are reading; the second has enabled us to look at it in detail. Both are valuable ways to avoid getting stuck in a rut. There are yet more methods, and we shall turn to them next.

seven
How Can I Go Deeper?

Do you want to take your Bible reading to a deeper level? Well, you don't need to go to theological college or anything like that, but there are three basic tools that will be an enormous help to you.

Acquire the Tools

The first is a concordance, a book where you can look up any word that appears in the Bible and find its reference. If you looked up "joy," for example, it would give you all the places where the word occurs in the Bible. I think it was Alexander Cruden, who lived nearly 300 years ago, who first compiled this valuable book. It was an amazing achievement to record each occurrence of every word in the King James version of the Bible without the aid of a computer! On top of that, Cruden suffered throughout his life from very bad health. We owe Mr. Cruden a great debt of gratitude. I am particularly thankful for his book (which has an honored place on my shelves) because I often half-remember snatches of the Bible in the King James version, on which I was brought up, and want to track them down.

Of course, the Cruden Concordance will be no use to you if you are using one of the modern translations of the Bible, so go to your nearest Christian bookseller (or search online) and find the appropriate concordance for your preferred version. This should make it easy for you to trace any reference you want to follow up in the Bible. We shall see below how useful this is.

A second very valuable Bible reading aid is a commentary. This tells you the authorship, background and circumstances of each of the Bible books and offers a commentary on it, which can be very illuminating, especially with some of the difficult bits.

The third book you will find useful is a Bible dictionary. This gives you detailed information about any subject mentioned in the Bible. There will be pages on "Egypt," for example, telling you about the history and customs of Egypt, since that country is often mentioned in the Bible. If you look up "book," it will tell you about the origins of writing, how the early books were made and so on. Suppose you wonder what a difficult Bible word such as "justification" really means, or what is known of an obscure person such as Demas—your Bible dictionary will help you out. Two such invaluable aids are the *New Bible Commentary* and the *New Bible Dictionary*, both published by IVP (InterVarsity Press). They have been compiled by good scholars, they have an enormous international circulation and you can rely on them. Reference books like these are not cheap, but that is what Christmas and birthdays are for! Drop the hint in the right place and the books may well materialize. If not, they are worth saving up for, as you will not regret buying them.

Now that we have the equipment to hand, how shall we proceed?

Study a Character

Biographies are always fascinating and the Bible is full of them. It does not tell us all we would like to know about the characters it portrays but it certainly offers us clear examples and warnings from their lives. As Paul tells us in his letter to the Romans, "Everything that was written in the past was written to teach us, so that through endurance and the encouragement of the Scriptures we might have hope" (Romans 15:4). The Old Testament books of Chronicles seem to have been specially written to teach important lessons to future generations through the lives they record. Many of these stories concern the kings of Israel and Judah. It is well worth first looking at the background to each story (that is where your commentary and dictionary may help), then at the steps God took to prepare the king for his life's work, then at how God used him, followed by the aftermath: did his later years show spiritual growth or decline? Each of these people leave us with some overall lesson to apply to our own lives.

Let us take an example from the New Testament. If you have read the Gospels, you may have noticed that most of the twelve apostles seem rarely to do anything as individuals. They are just "the Twelve," and all we know about them is their names. Andrew, for example, is just one of the list of names—except in John's Gospel. There he appears three times, and he is always introducing someone else to Jesus.

In chapter 1 he brings his brother Simon Peter to Jesus (v. 41). That was a pretty significant move, given that Peter was to become a great leader in the church! In chapter 6 we read of thousands of very hungry people hanging on Jesus' words. But how could they get anything to eat in the back of beyond, where there were no shops? It is Andrew who stumbles on the answer. He gets chatting to a boy who has a lunch bag of five barley cakes and two little fish, and introduces him to Jesus (vv. 8–9). The boy is willing to hand over his lunch, and Jesus miraculously transforms it into food for the whole multitude. This story is recorded in all four Gospels and is as certain as anything Jesus did, but it is easy to forget Andrew. If he had not introduced the lad to Jesus, the miracle would never have taken place.

The third occasion where Andrew appears in John's Gospel is in chapter 12, when some Greeks who have come to Jerusalem for the Passover festival are keen to meet Jesus. It is Andrew and Philip (both of them with Greek names, suggesting that they were at least familiar with that culture) who get alongside these Greeks and introduce them to Jesus (v. 22).

So we have only three little cameos of this man but each of them shows him doing the same thing. We are never told that he preached a sermon, but he clearly had a passion for bringing people into touch with Jesus. First, it was someone in his own family, then someone whom most people would not have bothered about, and then people who were outside the religious circles of the day. What an example for us!

Or think of Abraham, to whom Jews, Muslims and Christians all look back for inspiration. He was the first stirring example of how God deals with humankind and what he expects from us. God comes to Abraham in sheer love and offers to make him the father of many nations (Genesis 12:2; 15:5). The response he looks for is sheer faith—in Abraham and, indeed, in us. His faith is the main thing for which Abraham is remembered in the Bible. The Genesis account shows us four significant aspects of it.

- Abraham responded to God's call (Genesis 15:6). He entered into a personal trusting relationship with God. That is where true faith begins.
- Abraham obeyed God's command (12:1, 4). He left his country for an unknown destination, in trusting obedience to the God who had called him. Apart from one or two lapses, that obedience marked the whole of his subsequent life.
- Abraham looked to God's future (12:7; 17:3–8). He had no possessions whatsoever in the land of Canaan,

yet God had promised that he would be the father of many nations. God's promises proved to be a beacon of hope in the darkness.

- Abraham trusted God's faithfulness (15:6). He "believed the Lord" and God "credited it to him as righteousness." That faith was tested through and through. Tested by having no stake at all in Canaan although the land had been promised to him. Tested by having no children until well after he and his wife were too old (17:17). Tested by allowing his nephew Lot to choose the best land and relying on God to fulfill what he had undertaken (13:10–12).

Authentic faith is still marked by all four of those characteristics.

That is only skimming the surface of what Abraham's faith was, and what ours could be, but it gives enough of a foretaste, perhaps, to drive us into a fuller and more detailed study of this amazing man's life.

I wonder if you are intrigued by detective stories. The Bible offers you plenty of scope to do your own detective work. Luke is a good example. He was the author both of his Gospel and of the Acts of the Apostles, though he declines to attach his name to either. Clearly he was a self-effacing man. If we look him up in our concordance, what can we discover? Only three references. In his letter to the Colossians, Paul refers to "our dear friend Luke, the doctor" (4:14). The apostle had clearly benefited from the medical knowledge of this dear friend who was prepared willingly to enter prison with him. In Philemon 24 he is referred to as a "fellow worker"; his work for the gospel was not confined to his medical skill. And in 2 Timothy 4:11 we get a glimpse of his loyalty to Paul and the extent to which the apostle valued him, in the pathetic note "Only Luke is with me." Luke had accompanied Paul to his last imprisonment in Rome, from where that final letter was written.

That is all we can tell on the surface, but let us try reading between the lines. There are three places in his account in Acts where Luke slips from talking about "they" to "we." He is quietly informing us that he was there. The first place is in Acts 16:10–17. Luke turns up in Troas and accompanies Paul and his entourage to Philippi, where they conduct the first ever mission in Europe. This results in a small company of new believers—and the inference is that Luke stays with them, since the narrative then reverts to "they."

The next "we" passage begins several years later where the last one left off, in Philippi (20:5–21). It is not difficult to guess what Luke had been doing in those intervening years. He had been building up that little church at Philippi. It had grown to have its own "overseers and deacons" (Philippians 1:1) and Paul's letter shows how far the Christians" lives had progressed. If you had built up a church from almost nothing to that level, wouldn't you have mentioned it? I'm afraid I would—but not Luke! The third "we" passage is no less illuminating. It stretches from Acts 27:1 to 28:16. We leave Luke in Palestine at the end of the previous "we" section (21:17), and almost immediately Paul is practically lynched by the mob and spends two years in prison in Caesarea before he appeals to the emperor and is sent to Rome for trial. What was Luke doing in those two years? Surely he was gathering information for his Gospel. He tells us that he has researched it carefully (Luke 1:3). He would have had access to many of the main actors in the story of Jesus, including Jesus" mother, Mary. She is, doubtless, the source of Luke's accounts of Jesus' birth and childhood. And although Luke keeps himself rigorously out of the Gospel, we can discover a little about him from the events he decides to include. He chooses incidents that highlight women, Samaritans and Gentiles—outsiders, all of them. He underlines Jesus' love for the poor and his warnings against the seductions of wealth. He has much to say about the power of the Holy Spirit and of prayer in both his volumes. These must surely represent some of the concerns of Luke himself and enable us to see what sort of a man he was.

Finally, in his last "we" passage, Luke gives us a vivid account of a terrible sea journey, a shipwreck and their eventual arrival in Rome. There he leaves Paul in his own hired house, arguing the Christian case with all who come to see him—bound in body but free in spirit.

All of this is fair inference from what the text actually tells us and it makes a fascinating study. The Bible affords us plenty of others.

Examine a Chapter

Instead of reading a few verses, it is sometimes useful to examine a whole chapter. Take Romans 8, for example. In this marvelous chapter we find Paul laying before us the whole spread of salvation—past, present and future.

In verses 1–4, he dares to make the claim that "Therefore, there is now no condemnation for those who are in Christ Jesus' because his atoning death on the cross has cleared our debts and enables us to stand tall before God, knowing that our accusing past will never again be dragged up to shame us.

In the middle of the chapter, he concentrates on the present. Paul is not blind to our pains and adversities but he remains confident because of the presence of the Holy Spirit in each Christian life. It is the Spirit who assures us that we belong to God's family (v. 16), enables us to know him as Father (indeed, "Daddy" is what the Aramaic word Abba really means, v. 15), sets us free progressively from the downward pull of sin (v. 2), helps us to pray (v. 26) and cooperates with us in everything for our good (v. 28).

Consequently we can have every confidence as we face the future. God's plan is that we may be made like Jesus and live with him forever (vv. 29–30). So "If God is for us, who can be against us?" (v. 31). "Who shall separate us from the love of Christ? Shall trouble or hardship or persecution or famine or nakedness or danger or sword? ... No, in all these things we are more than conquerors through him who loved us" (vv. 35, 37).

Paul ends with a purple passage of confident faith and hope: "For I am convinced that neither death nor life… neither the present nor the future… nor anything else in all creation, will be able to separate us from the love of God that is in Christ Jesus our Lord" (vv. 38–39). What a chapter!

While not all chapters yield the riches of Romans 8, there are treasures to be found in lots of them. Take 2 Timothy 2, for instance. Here we see seven pen pictures of the Christian worker. Paul alludes to the role of the steward (a responsible official in a great house, who looks after the other servants, v. 2), the endurance of the soldier (v. 3), the self-discipline of the athlete (v. 5), the hard work of the farmer (v. 6), the craftsman's skill with his tools (v. 15), the cleanliness of tableware (v. 20) and the wholeheartedness of the servant or slave (v. 24). We all need those characteristics, and the broad overview of a chapter can sometimes prove particularly instructive.

Follow Up a Theme or a Word

There are many great themes running through the Bible: God's covenant mercies to his people, the faithful remnant in the midst of a fallen world, the kingdom of God, the justification of sinners, God's purposes for community life and so forth. Important topics such as family life, punishment and forgiveness, sexual behavior, marriage and singleness, work and money are all given extensive treatment in the Bible. It is instructive to gather up the teaching about them that you find in different parts of Scripture. Your concordance will be a real ally here, and you might even invest in a topical concordance, which deals not with individual words but with the subjects treated in the Bible.

So you can follow a theme, but you will often find it easier and just as fruitful to concentrate on a single significant word or phrase. I remember being much helped by a study I once did on "the will of God." I found that the Scriptures have quite a lot to say on the subject. I did another study on our "calling" and our "inheritance" and found it equally inspiring. "Take heed" was another one (based on the King James Bible). I must take heed of what sort of life I build on the only true foundation, Jesus himself (1 Corinthians 3:10). I need to take heed lest I fall, especially when I am feeling confident (1 Corinthians 10:12). I must take heed how I exercise my Christian liberty, in case it brings others into a new bondage (1 Corinthians 8:9) and must take heed to "complete the work" I have received from the Lord (Colossians 4:17). Daily I must take heed to let the light of Scripture dawn on my path (2 Peter 1:19). Following themes not only provides a comprehensive study for myself, but it gives me something to share with others if the opportunity arises.

I want to end this chapter by looking at the single word "able" and showing how its various occurrences can speak directly to the things people sometimes say about themselves and their Christian faith.

- *"I'm a hopeless case—if they knew what I am like inside…"*: Hebrews 7:25 speaks decisively to that fear. "He is able to save completely those who come to God through him, because he always lives to intercede for them."

- *"I think I am a committed Christian but I am not really sure God has accepted me"*: Here, 2 Timothy 1:12 is very helpful. "I am not ashamed, because I know whom I have believed, and am convinced that he is able to guard what I have entrusted to him."

- *"I am not convinced that prayer does any good"*: Ephesians 3:20–21 replies, "Now to him who is able to do immeasurably more than all we ask or imagine, according to his power that is at work within us, to him be glory in the church and in Christ Jesus throughout all generations."

- *"I'm so critical of other people"*: As Romans 14:4 reminds us, "Who are you to judge someone else's servants? To their own master they stand or fall. And they will stand, for the Lord is able to make them stand."

- *"I'm afraid to give as I should. I need financial security"*: "Remember this: Whoever sows sparingly will also reap sparingly, and whoever sows generously will also reap generously. Each of you should give what you have decided in your heart to give, not reluctantly or under compulsion, for God loves a cheerful giver. And God is *able* to make all grace abound to you, so that in all things at all times, having all that you need, you will abound in every good work" (2 Corinthians 9:6–8).

- *"My temptations overwhelm me. There seems no way out"*: But in Hebrews 2:18 we read, "Because he himself suffered when he was tempted, he is able to help those who are being tempted."

- *"This Christian life is so difficult. Will I ever make good?"*: "To him who is able to keep you from falling and to present you before his glorious presence without fault and with great joy...be glory...for evermore" (Jude 24–25).

Do you feel you could never have worked that out? Yes, you could! All I did was to take my concordance, find the references to "able" and apply them to the real world I have to live in. You can do the same. That is what the Bible is for.

eight
Why Not Read It With a Friend?

So far we have been thinking of Bible reading on our own. In the next two chapters I want to say something about reading it with others. First, let's see how a couple of friends can encourage one another enormously by reading some Scripture together on a regular basis.

The Importance of Personal Nurture

When someone has come to a clear decision to follow Christ, they very much need this sort of help. I vividly recall the early days of my own discipleship. I used to meet up once a week for half an hour or so with Richard Gorrie, the friend who had helped me to faith. He would suggest a passage of Scripture for us to read together. We would do so, turn some of our insights into prayer, and then I was free to raise any of the problems in my early Christian life that I wanted to share with him. To have an older Christian at hand like this was invaluable. It was a great way for me to learn to grow.

There is a real need for this sort of thing throughout the Christian community. Sadly, in many churches little attempt is made to introduce anyone at all to Christ: the church seems to be a club for insiders. Where there is a definite effort to win people to Christ, the follow-up is frequently very weak. New believers are expected to sink or swim in this new church environment, which may be quite alien to them. Singing hymns, seeing a church leader in operation, listening to prayers being read, listening to sermons that make assumptions not shared by the newcomer—all this may be quite outside his or her experience. Clearly, new Christians need some gentle tuition in the new life on which they have embarked.

Mercifully, the Alpha Course has proved invaluable as an introduction to discipleship, but that is a group affair and tends not to provide the intimacy of the one-to-one session. Suppose you are learning to use a computer. You only have to ask yourself whether you gain more from being part of a whole class, or whether you do better with someone sitting alongside you. I know what helps me most.

Because of this lack of personal nurturing, a great many converts to the faith never get the grounding they need. The mature believers hope they will get stuck in and grow, and some do, but many fall by the wayside because no disciplined effort has been made to mentor them. One of the greatest things we can do for a new believer is to have a number of sessions with him or her, reading carefully chosen passages of the Bible together, praying things over and allowing any of the problems that are inevitable in the early stages of discipleship to surface. I dread to think where I would be now if Richard had not taken that trouble with me.

Right, how shall we go about it? Let us suppose that your friend Sam has come to the point in his life when he is ready to entrust his life to Christ, and that you are the one who has been the last link in the chain bringing him to that point. It is your responsibility to help him to get his sea legs on the ship of faith. He is going to need help, particularly if, like most people these days, he has had no Christian background. Other people will doubtless teach him a lot, but he will have a special bond with you because you led him to the Lord. The apostle Paul was well aware of the power of that link. He wrote to the Corinthians, "Even though you have ten thousand guardians in Christ, you do not have many fathers, for in Christ Jesus I became your father through the gospel" (1 Corinthians 4:15). Your relationship with him as a "father" will be unique, and you must make good use of it, for he will take advice and guidance from you that he might spurn from anyone else.

The Time Together

You will naturally suggest to your friend Sam that you get together soon after he has fumbled his way to some sort of commitment. That is one of the most critical times of all, when doubts fester, he is not sure what he has done and the pull of the old life is strong. So arrange to meet him soon. Have a Bible for yourself and bring one along for him too, in case he has not got one.

The First Session

In this first time together you will want one thing to become crystal clear—that this act of commitment to Christ is no bizarre oddity, as Sam may be feeling, but an essential for all Christians. So choose a passage that illustrates that act of surrender and new life. Three good ones are the story of Zacchaeus (Luke 19:1–10), the story of Nicodemus (John 3:1–18) and the story of the conversion of Saul of Tarsus (Acts 9:1–25). Suppose we choose the third of these.

You will each turn to the passage, pray for insight and read it through. Make sure Sam reads at least half the passage, so as to get used to the sound of his own voice reading the Bible. Then suggest a couple of minutes of complete silence as each of you looks for some helpful thought that can be shared with the other. It would be wise for you to give the lead after those two minutes are over: "I loved verse 8 and the way Saul changed from being a macho leader, anxious to beat up the Christians in Damascus, to allowing others to lead him into the place—once God had started changing him. I wonder whether you have noticed any changes yet in your own experience?" He will say if he has noticed anything of the kind yet, and you might ask him, "What bit of the passage did you like most as you read it through, and why?" Always ensure that you are both trying to see what it meant in the original situation and then how that can apply to your own lives. As we saw in Chapter 4, both are necessary.

What you want Sam to see from this first session is that God can change the life of the most determined opponent: conversion is perfectly natural and very common. You want him to see also that, although we may not go through the same psychological sequences as Saul, and although our coming to faith may be much less spectacular and more gradual than his, four elements in Saul's conversion hold good for everyone. First, Saul came to recognize that he was in the wrong for persecuting Christians (v. 4). Second, he came to recognize Jesus as the Lord of glory (v. 5). Third, he made an act of surrender to him (vv. 6–9), and fourth, his subsequent life showed the difference. Some of those differences seem to have been almost immediate. He began to tell others (v. 20), he grew spiritually (v. 22) and he abandoned his old behavior pattern (v. 21). He discovered Christian fellowship with Ananias, his "brother," whom only a few days earlier he would have thrown into prison, and accepted ministry from him (v. 17). He was baptized and filled with the Holy Spirit (v.

18) and he tasted the first signs of opposition from those who used to be his colleagues (v. 23).

These are some of the truths that you will want your friend to discover. It does not matter if you do not discuss them all. It matters enormously, though, that he begins to find that the Bible is a book that speaks to him, begins to pick verses and apply them to his life, and begins to talk to you without embarrassment about spiritual things. You may want to prompt him by directing his attention to a particular verse so that he discovers its truths for himself. Could he say, like Saul, that he has begun to see who Jesus really is? Has his conscience, like Saul's, been pricked into repentance? Has he fallen at the feet of Jesus in surrender? Has he begun to notice any difference in his life? Is he aware of the Holy Spirit's presence inside him? You might even turn to Romans 8:15, where he can see that the first job of the Spirit when he takes up residence in new believers is to assure them that they belong in God's family.

By a judicious mixture of contributing some of these thoughts yourself and asking your friend what he reckons a particular verse means, you will cover most of the main points in the stirring passage and he will be able to see that there is nothing odd about the surrender to Christ that he has made. He is simply following the greatest of the apostles.

You will then probably want to suggest a short time of prayer. To get started, suggest that neither of you uses more than one sentence, that you speak in your own natural words (not attempting any high-flown "religious" jargon) and that you turn a thought that each of you has found helpful while reading the Bible into a one-sentence prayer or "thank you." Start off yourself, so that you can model the prayer for him: "Verse 15: Thank you, Lord, so much that you have called Sam, like Saul long ago, to be a chosen instrument for you to carry your name before others. Amen"; or "Verse 10: 'The Lord called to Ananias.' Lord, make both of us really sensitive to your voice when you want us to do something for you, just as Ananias was."

Sam will soon break the sound barrier and follow your example in prayer. If he bursts out, "I can't pray!" you might gently respond, "Yes, you can. You can talk to me, so you can talk to the Lord. He has promised to be among us when two or three gather in his name. Tell him what is on your heart." In my experience, that almost always liberates new believers to start praying aloud, which is something they are going to find valuable during their Christian lives.

That is quite enough input for your first session. There needs to be time for relaxed conversation, and for Sam to bring up anything that is troubling him. It has been an important "first": the first time he has read a passage of the Bible in this way; the first time he has done so with another person; the first time he has commented on it aloud and prayed about it with someone else; the first time he has realized that this business of Christian commitment is not a strange fixation of some wacky Christians but is the key to being a Christian disciple. In addition, he has begun to discover how to read the Bible so that it speaks to him, and he can make good use of that in his own time with God before you meet again. You have laid the foundation of a devotional life.

Subsequent meetings on a regular basis could profitably cover a range of topics that are essential to Christian life and growth.

The Second Session

This could focus on Christian assurance. It would be good to read 1 John 5:9–21. You would want to get across the truth that if we accept human testimony, it is crazy, and very insulting, to doubt God's testimony when he tells us that he has given us eternal life and that this life is in his Son. "Those who have the Son have life; those who do not have the Son of God do not have life" (v. 12). How black and white it is! You ask your friend, "Have you received Jesus, God's Son, into your life?" He says, "Yes, I think I have." In that case, God assures him that he already has life that can never end and he is meant to know it (v. 13). You could point to the further assurance to be found in the experience of answered prayer (v. 15), progressive victory over sin as the Son of God keeps him safe (v. 18), increasing understanding of Jesus (v. 20) and a determination to keep Christ in the number one slot in life (v. 21).

The Third Session

This could well be on Bible reading. You might choose Acts 8:26–40, all about Philip and the Ethiopian official. You might have such questions as these in the back of your mind as you try to help Sam to see the power and importance of the Bible in his life: "What was the traveler doing as he rode along? Why did he need help? How exactly did Philip help him? What might be today's equivalent of that? What effect did his dawning understanding of God's truth have on the Ethiopian's life? Where does the Holy Spirit come into all this?" Such questions, suitably dispersed throughout your Bible reading time, will certainly help Sam to get to the heart of the passage, and will be a model for the sort of questions he may ask himself during his own times of Bible reading.

The Fourth Session

This could be on prayer, and one of the most helpful passages in the whole Bible about prayer is Colossians 1:3–14. The questions you want Sam to reflect on are something like these: "What are the main things for which Paul thanks God in the lives of these people he has never met? Why is thanksgiving such an important part of prayer? How should we pray for our friends? Paul prays that they may know God's power: what sort of things is that power meant to achieve? What are the main marks of Christian discipleship in this passage?"

The Fifth Session

How about doing something on the church, the corporate expression of the Christian life? Maybe Romans 12:1–13 would be a good passage to examine. Questions such as these might be in your mind as you ask yourself what important lessons Sam needs to learn about the church from this passage of Scripture: "What does true worship involve? The church is Christ's body on earth: what implications flow from this? How do you see them in your local church? If 'each member belongs to all the others' (5), what does this mean for our relationships as Christians? According to Paul, we all have different gifts and abilities. What do you think yours are? Are you using them for the benefit of the Christian community? What practical results are mentioned here as flowing from wholehearted surrender to the Lord? Ask yourself if anything is holding you back from offering your body as a living sacrifice" (1).

The Sixth Session

It is time to look at the issue of temptation and victory. Luke 4:1–13 would be a good passage, and the thoughts you might want to see explored from the text are these: "What were the temptations that pressed on Jesus? What would they look like in our day? Is there anything significant about the time and place when those temptations struck? Jesus quoted various Scriptures when handling his temptations, and this proved highly effective.

His quotes come from Deuteronomy 8:3, 6:13 and 6:16. What do you learn from that? Have you learned yet to use promises of Scripture as weapons against temptation? Don't you think the first and last sentences of this passage are highly significant?"

The Seventh Session

As a final session, it is a good idea to look outwards to the whole area of Christian service. A helpful passage might be Acts 5:40—6:8, and questions like these should prove stimulating: "What motivated these people to serve the Lord? How about you? How many forms of service are mentioned here? Are the 'spiritual' jobs more important than the practical ones? How is it that the disciples 'increased rapidly' in Jerusalem? What are you doing now that you might not be doing if you were not a Christian?"

It is impossible to exaggerate the impact that a few sessions of Bible reading like these will have on new Christians. It will open their eyes to some of the main aspects of the Christian life. It will give them a taste of close Christian fellowship. It will ensure their growth, and it will provide a pattern for their own devotional times and a forum for them to raise questions and get some answers. Finally, it will be an enormous encouragement to you personally to find yourself able to help your friends to grow in grace and in the knowledge of the Lord and Savior, Jesus Christ.

nine

How About a Bible Study Group?

Bible Study Groups Are Needed

If the Bible is right in regarding Christians as limbs in the body of Christ, it is obvious that we need each other, and this applies as much in the matter of Bible reading as it does in any other aspect of life. If "each member belongs to all the others" (Romans 12:5), then we need to find a way of expressing and deepening that interdependence. The Bible study group can be an excellent way. There is real value in sitting with a group of friends and studying a bit of the Bible together, all of you sharing your insights and building one another up. More than that, you share something of your lives and aspirations, disappointments and joys. Room must be made for this human sharing of life and experience if the group is to gel as a close fellowship of Christians and not just a reading group.

You may not feel you could offer leadership in such a group yourself but that need not stop you initiating it. Members of the group could take it in turn to lead for an evening so that everyone has a go. After all, it is not as if you are being asked to preach a sermon. You are merely chairing the discussion for an evening among a group of friends.

I recall a conversation I once had with George Gallup, the inventor of the famous Gallup polls. He told me what he did when he got the idea of a group like this. He called up twelve men he knew and invited them. Ten of them said "Yes," and that began the small group involvement which has, over many years, been a great enrichment to his life and the lives of his friends. It could be the same for you.

Sadly, many churches do not have anything of the kind. Perhaps the minister is suspicious of goings-on among a bunch of amateur Bible readers in a private home when he or she is not present. Some ministers feel that they should be the ones giving Bible teaching, in a sermon or a midweek meeting. For whatever reason, the minister may discourage small group Bible study. This is a real shame because it is one of the great ways for people to grow in understanding their faith. And remember, you don't have to ask permission from a minister or anyone else to have such a group in your own home. So why not see if there are people in your neck of the woods who would like to enrich their spiritual diet in this way?

The Impact of Such a Group

There is a massive ignorance of the Bible these days. It is the bestseller that nobody reads, and yet, as we have seen, it has tremendous impact on the character of those who make it the foundation of their lives. Over the years, I have heard many testimonies to its power. Mr. Dzapasi was a witch doctor in Zimbabwe before he ended up in prison. Thanks to the Bible and the personal care of the Prison Fellowship, he became a fully trained pastor. "It was one day after the Prison Fellowship members had visited me in my cell and shared the word of God with me that I was saved," he said. Before long he started a Bible study group with some of the other prisoners. "I was even happy to serve my sentence, and actually felt it was not long enough, considering what I had done to God. Prison officers could not believe the change in me, and were astonished when I started preaching the gospel to fellow inmates and even to them!"

In the same country, a man called Munyoro was awaiting the death sentence but found peace with God and the comfort of the Scriptures. He testified, "The pain and terror of the death sentence was made lighter when I accepted the Messiah as the center of my life. I began to read the Bible, prayed, and sang to the glory of God."

A Chinese student, Yan Rong Hui, tells how "God's word was our food during the Cultural Revolution." Her father was arrested for being in a Christian meeting. All the Bibles in the area were confiscated—but one escaped notice. This was used by many people, her own family included. "Some of the psalms were copied out for me to read and every day I read some verses. But I asked the Lord to give me a Bible—and he enabled me to procure one from a friend of my mother's. The Bible passages were very useful to our family as we gathered to read them. We had much trouble during the Cultural Revolution, but the word of God gave our family strength to face these troubles and to overcome them."

Enough said. The Bible has enormous life-changing power. We need to read it on our own but we can also gain immeasurably from reading it with others and learning from them.

Leading a Group

Bad leadership ruins many a group! Inadequate leaders are often late in starting, have not prepared beforehand and talk too much themselves. They cannot restrain the overtalkative or encourage the timid. They ask questions to which the answers are obvious, and then provide the answers themselves. They allow the meeting to drift on far too long, they manage to cover only part of the passage, and nothing is summarized, applied or prayed about.

Good leaders are unostentatious, asking questions only when discussion dries up, and then very shrewdly and humbly. They keep to the passage and so avoid waffle. They gently insist on the application of Scripture to daily life and discourage glibness by pressing for further explanation. They defuse argument, keep the atmosphere sweet and encourage the shy. Good leaders are essentially encouragers, who direct operations from the rear. They make all the difference to whether the members go away feeling they have had a wasted evening or a fulfilling time of learning and fellowship.

Obviously, leaders need to ensure that there is agreement beforehand about what method of Bible study is to be used and what passage is to be studied. It might be a study course going through a book of the Bible. It might be an examination of what the Bible has to say on an important topic. It might be looking at selected passages. The important thing is that the leaders themselves are well prepared. There are three vital ingredients in preparation. First, they will need to have prayed about the passage and the people who will be coming to the meeting. Second, they will need to have soaked themselves in the passage. That will probably have included some work with a commentary: the New International Version Study Bible is an invaluable ally. Third, they will need to have given some thought to how they will handle discussion on the day. They will want to put people at ease, cultivate a worshipful attitude and ensure that all get a chance to participate. They will seek to avoid the dullness of a dry academic discussion and to encourage the group to apply what they read to their personal lives and maybe to their activities as a group as well.

In point of fact, many of the best groups find that their study together leads to common action for the good of others. They might, for example, read the first few verses of James chapter 5, about the dangers of wealth and the selfishness it can breed—and decide as a result to offer to redecorate the house of an elderly widow nearby. They might be reading a passage in the prophet Micah or Amos about social justice, and this could lead them to make representations about a local issue before the town council. It is not the responsibility of the leader to come up with ideas like this—they may spring from any member of the group—but the leader will want to ensure that the Scripture is applied, and will be open to practical suggestions as to how that can be achieved.

The Art of Asking Questions

Part of the leader's preparation will be to think up suitable questions to help people grapple with the passage or topic under consideration. Good questions stimulate discussion and help people to discover important truths that are being overlooked. But questioning is not as simple as it sounds. Here are a few suggestions.

Avoid questions that are obscure, or to which the answer is obvious. Your aim is to open up discussion. It is a good idea to use "What?" "How?" or "Why?" questions. They will probably have more than one answer, and this enables plenty of participation. Don't provide the answer yourself!

Do not be content with scratching the surface. A supplementary question can help, such as "What do others think?" or "What might that mean for us?"

You may find it useful to set one or two questions in advance. This will, of course, involve you in preparing further ahead. Suppose you were studying Matthew 6: two good questions, which could prove very fruitful in discussion, would be "What false attitudes does Jesus condemn here?" and "What attitude does he advocate?"

If you were looking at the Lord's Prayer, a good question to set beforehand might be "Analyze the Lord's Prayer and suggest how you can use it as a framework for your own prayers." Or, if you were looking at the mission of the Twelve in Matthew 9:36—10:20, you could ask, "What principles in this passage are appropriate (a) only to the apostles, (b) to mission outreaches today, and (c) to the lives of all Christians?"

Be shrewd, humble and focused in your questions. Keep before the group the two essential questions that we mentioned earlier: "What did this mean to the original people involved?" and "If that was the case, how does it apply to us?" In that way you will avoid pious thoughts that have no relation to the real meaning of the passage on the one hand, and academic observations that have no relation to life on the other.

The Bible Study Itself

It is good to start with a meal if possible, in order to allow people to leave behind the pressures of the day, relate to one another and prepare for what is to come. If a meal is impossible, coffee is the next best thing. If you are leading for the evening, it might be good to move next into some worshipful songs, especially if you have an instrumentalist. In any case, have some silence before God so that you can all get into the attitude of attentively coming to meet him. You are after much the same thing in the group study as you were in the one-to-one sessions described in the last chapter. You will give a very short introduction, not parading all the understanding you have gained in your preparation but keeping it under wraps in case it is needed in the discussion period.

It is important to make it crystal clear how you want the group to proceed. If, for example, you have set them a question or two beforehand, it might be good to say, "We shall not read the passage tonight, but contribute one by one our reflections on the first question." Or you might say, "Let's each try, as we look at this passage tonight, to find something for the head, something for the heart and something for the feet." That's as much as to say that understanding, devotion and practical action should go hand in hand.

If you have decided to do a topical study, such as bringing up children or the use of money, the leader's preparation will be multiplied. But they will not parade it: that would inhibit discussion. Instead, they will use it to choose particular verses in different parts of the Bible that bear on the subject, and then give each member a slip of paper with a Scripture reference on it. The group members will then look up their verses and read them out, and the ensuing discussion will be lively and cohesive because the verses will have been chosen to give a good overview of the Bible's teaching on the matter.

In the discussion, let people contribute freely, but you will need to be vigilant. There is always the overtalkative member who, in effect, silences many of the others. Watch out for them! It is easy enough to smile graciously and say, "Good, John, but could we hear from someone else first, who hasn't had a chance to chip in yet?," perhaps adding, "Jenny, how does it strike you?"

There are sure to be some silent members. It is wise to let them take their time, just sitting and taking it all in. But maybe after a couple of sessions you could draw them out with a judicious question directed to them personally: "Andy, what did you like most about this passage?"

In a Bible study group composed of long-standing Christians, there is a danger of glibness, of the parrot-like repetition of Christian technical words like "Eucharist" and "salvation." Try to pierce the religious crust! If, for example, one group was commenting on the wickedness of humankind in general, based on Ephesians 2:1, you might gently say, "That's quite true, Richard, but it also applies to every one of us, doesn't it? I wonder if you would be good enough to change it into the first person and read it to us again?" After a moment's incomprehension, he would slowly read, "As for me, I was dead in my transgressions and sins, in which I used to live when I followed the ways of the world." At that point, glibness tends to evaporate!

Some will be sure to come up with irrelevant comments. You

want gently to get their noses back into the text so that they are not imposing their own ideas on to it but struggling to uncover what is actually there. Questions such as, "Yes, Sarah, but what verse do you see that in?" is generally effective.

And then there will be the mistaken comment. Rescue anything you can from it but suggest, "Does it, I wonder, rather mean…? What do others think?"

You are likely to have had an excellent evening. End with prayer, perhaps in the group as a whole, encouraging everyone to utter short prayers or praises. Maybe, if the group is large, split people up into threes to pray, and end with a final song or the Lord's Prayer. Sometimes personal needs will have arisen in the discussion and these call for prayer. Sometimes silence is the most fitting response to God's word.

Bible study in small groups can be one of the most effective building blocks of a growing, informed and participatory congregation. It is an opportunity too good to miss.

ten
Can I Trust the Bible?

As we end this book, we need to return to the question we glanced at earlier. Can I rely on the Bible? If I trust it, will it let me down? What about all the problems I find there? Why should I regard it any more highly than other books? In a word, why regard it as authoritative for my belief and behavior?

The Statements of the Churches

The churches of the world are almost unanimous in regarding the Bible as the supreme authority in the Christian faith. Of course, church tradition and human reason are also important, but the ultimate authority must go to the Scriptures. The Lambeth Conference of Anglican bishops from across the world debated this matter fully in 1958 and came up with this statement:

The Church is not over the Scriptures, but under them in the sense that the process of canonization was not one whereby the Church conferred authority on the books, but one whereby the Church acknowledged them to possess authority. And why? The books were recognized as giving the witness of the apostles to the life, teaching, death and resurrection of the Lord, and the interpretation by the apostles of these events. To that apostolic teaching the Church must ever bow.

The language is slightly dated but the point is well made—and, in theory at least, the churches do bow to that authority.

The Roman Catholic Church defined its position at the 16th-century Council of Trent as follows: "This Synod, following the example of the ancient fathers, receives and venerates all the books of the Old and New Testament, seeing that one God is the author of both."

The worldwide Lutheran Church makes much the same claim in its Formula of Concord: "The Holy Scriptures alone remain the only judge, rule and standard according to which all dogmas shall be discerned and judged."

The Presbyterian Churches have as their official statement of belief the Westminster Confession, which states, "All the books of the Old and New Testament are given by inspiration of God, to be the rule of faith and life."

The Anglican Church, too, defined its position clearly in the

Thirty-Nine Articles. The sixth Article expressly states, "Holy Scripture containeth all things necessary for salvation: so that whatsoever is not read therein nor may be proved thereby is not to be required of any man that it should be believed as an article of faith." Even today (despite all sorts of strange beliefs you will find among some clergy), that remains the Anglican position. Whenever Anglican clergy change jobs, they have to make a solemn declaration to the congregation of their "firm and sincere belief" in the "faith uniquely set forth in the holy Scriptures." Indeed, no one can be ordained unless, in response to the bishop's question, they can reply, "I accept the holy Scriptures as revealing all things necessary for eternal salvation through faith in Christ." The candidate is presented with a New Testament by the bishop, who says, "Receive this book, as a sign of the authority given you this day to preach and speak God's word to his people. Build them up in his truth and serve them in his name."

It is plain, then, that the avowed intention of the universal Church is to give the highest authority to the Bible, believing that it derives from God's self-revelation. Now that is a remarkable claim. Where did it come from?

The Attitude of Jesus to the Scriptures

Of course, Jesus only had the Old Testament, but his attitude to it is a clear example to us of how we should regard the Bible as a whole.

He studied it carefully and framed his life in accordance with it.

It was in the Old Testament that Jesus saw his role as the Messiah, Son of God, Son of Man and Suffering Servant. He realized that his healings, parables, suffering, death and resurrection were all foreshadowed in those same Scriptures, not to mention his virgin birth in Bethlehem. His teaching, too, was rooted in obedience to and fulfillment of the Old Testament. The Sermon on the Mount makes that very plain.

He regarded it as inspired by God.

Jesus saw God himself as the ultimate author behind the human writers. How else can we understand Mark 12:36: "David himself, speaking by the Holy Spirit, declared..."? When rebuking the Sadducees for their unbelief, he says, "But about the resurrection, have you not read what God said to you...?," quoting Exodus 3:6. It would be easy to multiply examples of this attitude, such as John 17:12: "None has been lost except the one doomed to destruction so that Scripture would be fulfilled" or Matthew 26:54: "But how then would the Scriptures be fulfilled that say it must happen in this way?" Perhaps the most remarkable example of Jesus' own confidence in the divine origin of Scripture comes in Matthew 19:4–5. Here he is quoting the words of Genesis 2:24, which in themselves are a comment made by the author of Genesis, and Jesus ascribes them to God himself: "Haven't you read that at the beginning the Creator 'made them male and female,' and said…?" Clearly, Jesus regarded this statement by the author of Genesis as nothing less than spoken by God, even though the Genesis account does not directly attribute it to God. The inference is clear: for Jesus, a word of Scripture was a word of God.

He regarded Scripture as absolutely authoritative.

In Matthew 5:17–18, from which Jesus goes on to interpret the Old Testament and enlarge on its teaching, he says, "Do not think that I have come to abolish the Law or the Prophets; I have not come to abolish them but to fulfill them. I tell you the truth, until heaven and earth disappear, not the smallest letter, not the least stroke of a pen, will by any means disappear from the Law until everything is accomplished." In controversial discussions with the theologians of his day, Jesus would constantly go back to the Scriptures for his authority. Was it the question of life after death? To the Scriptures they must go, and the Sadducees' error lay in their failure to do so (Mark 12:24). Was it a question of what might or might not be done on the sabbath day? To the Scripture he would go, basing his argument and his practice on biblical precedent (Matthew 12:3–5). His attitude was clear and consistent: "The Scripture cannot be broken" (John 10:35). The reason was very clear to him. The Scriptures embodied God's revelation and therefore, of course, they were stamped with the authority of God. Even though Jesus claimed to embody in his own person the ultimate authority of God, we never find him opposing his own authority to that of Scripture. He had not come to destroy but to fulfill. This attitude is found in every strand of his teaching and remained unchanged throughout his life. We find it in his first sermon at Nazareth; we find it in his teaching after the resurrection.

So that is the first and greatest reason why Christians revere the Bible, seek to understand it, obey it and allow their lives to be molded by it. This was the attitude of their Master, Jesus Christ. It is hard to call Jesus your Lord and at the same time rubbish his attitude to Scripture. If he who possessed all knowledge revered it as God's word, so should we.

The Intrinsic Power of the Scriptures

Christians do not treasure the Scriptures as normative simply because of what the churches say or even because that was clearly the attitude of Jesus. They trust the Bible because it works. Time and again in this book I have quoted people whose lives have been changed by the Scriptures. Here are one or two more examples to emphasize the point.

David Suchet, the English actor best known for playing the title role in the TV drama Poirot, tells how he was lying in his bath in an American hotel when he had an impulsive desire to read the Bible. He found a Gideon Bible in his room and started to read the New Testament. As he read, he entrusted his life to Jesus Christ. "From somewhere I got this desire to read the Bible. That was the most important part of my conversion...

In the New Testament I suddenly discovered the way that life should be followed."

Abraham Lincoln maintained, "All the good from the Savior of the world is communicated to us through this book. But for this book we could not know right from wrong. All the things desirable to man are in it." Another American President, Woodrow Wilson, wrote in much the same vein: "When you read the Bible, you will know it is the word of God because you will have found it the key to your own heart, your own happiness and your own duty." Stanley Baldwin, once the British Prime Minister, observed, "The Bible is high explosive...It has startled the individual soul in ten thousand different places into a new life, a new world, a new faith." That is what has persuaded so many people of its divine origin. They have read it and sensed its intrinsic authority and inspiration.

The Bible has Authority to Inform the Mind

Ours is an age of vast ignorance about the Christian faith. We need to be informed, and no information is as reliable as the primary source book, the Bible. Ours is an age of unparalleled heresies about the Christian faith. We need to be informed so that we can stand firm. The Bible provides that information. Ours is an age where new sects constantly emerge, claiming to be true to the Bible. They rely on our remaining uninformed about what the Scriptures actually teach. The Bible provides the remedy.

Could you lead someone to Christian faith from the Scriptures? Could you find the Lord's Prayer or the Ten Commandments? We may be very intelligent and good at our jobs but at the same time very ignorant in this area. Scripture has the authority of a teacher, to dispel our ignorance.

It Has Authority to Touch the Conscience

When we read the Bible with an open heart, we often feel challenged, rebuked, corrected. It is like a doctor telling us we are overweight or a dentist probing at decay in our tooth. That's the sort of authority it has—and I need it. In this pluralist age where anything goes, in this relativist society where there are no agreed standards, I need an anchor. I need to hear the oracles of God and allow his word to challenge and change me. Don't you?

It Has Authority to Build Character

One of the most remarkable moral phenomena of the past 50 or so years has been the way the Scriptures have sustained believers in China, Cuba and other totalitarian countries where the most determined efforts, backed up by torture and execution, have been made to change the lifestyles and beliefs of humanity into an ideology devised by the state authorities. This has failed miserably. If we wonder how the Christian believers have been able to withstand the immense pressure brought on them, the answer is not hard to find. It has been through the Bible. That has been their most precious possession. They cannot comprehend how little we in the free world value it. The toughness and resilience of their character has been formed by this book, and all the might of anti-Christian states has been unable to destroy the Church because its faith and practice has been built on the Bible.

A while ago, I heard this fascinating example of the life-changing power of the Bible. A bandit in Latin America captured an itinerant bookseller and ordered him to burn his Bibles. "May I read a bit before they are burnt?" asked the Christian. The bandit reluctantly agreed, and the bookseller read him 1 Corinthians 13. "Don't burn that. Give it to me," said the bandit. Then he read Psalm 23 and the story of the good Samaritan. The response was the same. As a result, none of the Bibles were destroyed and in due course the bandit was converted and became a Christian minister. D. L. Moody was surely right in saying, "Either sin will keep you from this book or this book will keep you from sin."

A second story is an equally powerful example of the life-changing power of the Bible. In 1984, Dr. Steve Harris, a chiropractor in Houston, who had prayed earnestly for the Lord to use him, gave a copy of the Bible to a difficult and dissolute patient, Bill Last. Six weeks later, Last was murdered. A year previously, Last's daughter Deborah had been brutally murdered with a pickaxe by Karla Faye Tucker, who was duly convicted of the crime, confined on Death Row and finally executed in controversial circumstances in February 1998. But while she was in prison the Scriptures had led her to a thoroughgoing conversion, which made her a blessing to all the prisoners around her. She refused to plead for pardon but faced her death with great peace. Meanwhile, in 1990, Ron Carlson, Last's son, found himself idly thumbing through the Bible that Harris had given to his father. Scornful and full of hate at first (Deborah had virtually brought him up and had been very close to him), he became captured by the power of the Bible's message and became a Christian.

A couple of years later, Ron Carlson did the hardest thing in his life: he went to see the imprisoned Karla Faye and told her he forgave her for what she had done to his sister. Together they wept at the feet of the Lord who had accepted them both and made new people of them. Indeed, they became friends, and Carlson petitioned for Faye's reprieve. When that failed, she asked him if he would witness her execution, not on behalf of her victim but on her own behalf. Incredibly difficult though that was, he did it, and today he lives in Houston working as a machine operator. He spends his spare time working for the abolition of the death penalty and ministering to Death Row inmates. He offers them the new life in Christ to which the Scriptures point, a life that can give inner liberation even on Death Row. How fruitful Steve Harris's gift of a Bible, 15 years earlier, has been!

Those are the two main reasons why I, at least, accept the full inspiration and authority of the Bible. First, because Jesus did, and I am his follower; and second, because of the impact it makes on my life, the life of my friends who read it, and the lives of those to whom I spread its message. So may I ask you two questions as I close?

- Will you determine to read the Scriptures reverently and expectantly?
- Will you seek to put into practice what you read?

A wise Christian leader was once asked, "Which is the best translation of the Bible?" He replied, "The translation into practice." He was right.